Roundabouts
The sky above us

Kate Petty
and Jakki Wood

A & C Black • London

First published 1993
A & C Black (Publishers) Limited
35 Bedford Row
London WC1R 4JH

ISBN 0-7136-3711-0

© Aladdin Books Limited 1993
An Aladdin Book
designed and produced by
Aladdin Books Limited
28 Percy Street
London
WIP 9FF

A CIP catalogue record for this book
is available from the British Library

Printed in Belgium

Design David West
Children's Book Design
Illustration Jakki Wood
Text Kate Petty
Consultants Keith Lye B.A., F.R.S.G.,
Eva Bass Cert. Ed., teacher of
geography to 5-8 year-olds

Contents

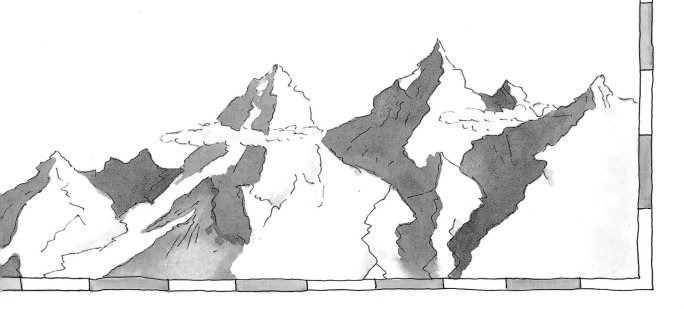

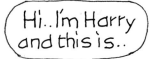

The air above us

Harry and Ralph load the basket of their balloon with tanks of fuel. Today, they want to climb high in the sky to explore the air above. Around the Earth there is a layer of air called the atmosphere. Without the atmosphere, we would have no air to breathe and no protection from the heat of the Sun.

Earth

Atmosphere

Space

Going up

There's a big burst of flames and the hot air inside the balloon lifts them off the ground.

Up they go, above the houses...

and the trees...

above the town...

above the hills and the mountains.

As the balloon rises, the air becomes thinner. Ralph has an oxygen pack just in case he has trouble breathing.

Brrrr... it's chilly up here!

How do I look?

High up in the sky, it's cold. Harry has lots of blankets. Harry and Ralph can't go any higher in their balloon but they are still in the lowest layer of the atmosphere, called the troposphere. The troposphere can stretch up to 18 kilometres above the Earth.

Above the weather

Harry and Ralph are about 4km above the ground. Their balloon is buffeted about by the wind. Dark storm clouds are approaching. Harry wishes they could fly higher, to the stratosphere. The stratosphere is above the clouds and the weather.

There's another balloon up there.

It's a weather balloon with no people on board so it can go very high.

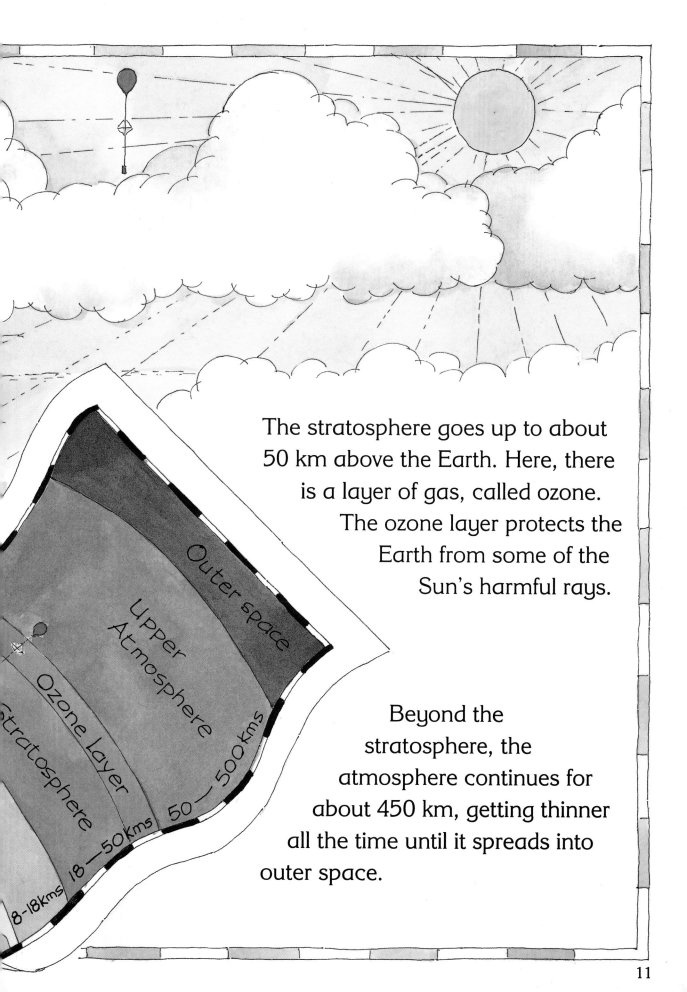

The stratosphere goes up to about 50 km above the Earth. Here, there is a layer of gas, called ozone. The ozone layer protects the Earth from some of the Sun's harmful rays.

Beyond the stratosphere, the atmosphere continues for about 450 km, getting thinner all the time until it spreads into outer space.

Outer space

Upper Atmosphere

Ozone Layer

Stratosphere

50 — 500 kms

18 — 50 Kms

8-18 kms

Clouds

It's time for the picnic. Harry pours two hot cups of tea from the thermos flask. Little clouds of steam rise from their cups. Ralph is looking for the biscuits, when suddenly …

they are in the middle of a cloud. The cloud is like the steam from their tea.

I can't see a thing.

Those water droplets are ganging up on us!

Fog and mist are clouds on the ground.

When water is heated, an invisible gas comes off the surface. This is called water vapour. Air contains lots of water vapour. As air rises to a cooler level, water vapour turns back into tiny droplets of water. The droplets are so small and light they float about in the air. Clouds are made from millions of tiny water droplets.

The next time someone boils a kettle in your home, stand well back and watch the steam rise. If there is a window nearby, what happens to it?

Rain, rain

Ralph starts to think the trip is a big mistake because the next cloud he sees is a rain cloud.

Inside the cloud, tiny droplets of water are moving about, bumping into one another and making bigger and bigger drops. When the drops become fat and heavy, they fall to the ground as rain. Harry puts on his anorak.

There's no getting away from the water cycle.

Harry looks through the rain to the ground below. He can see a river running into the sea.

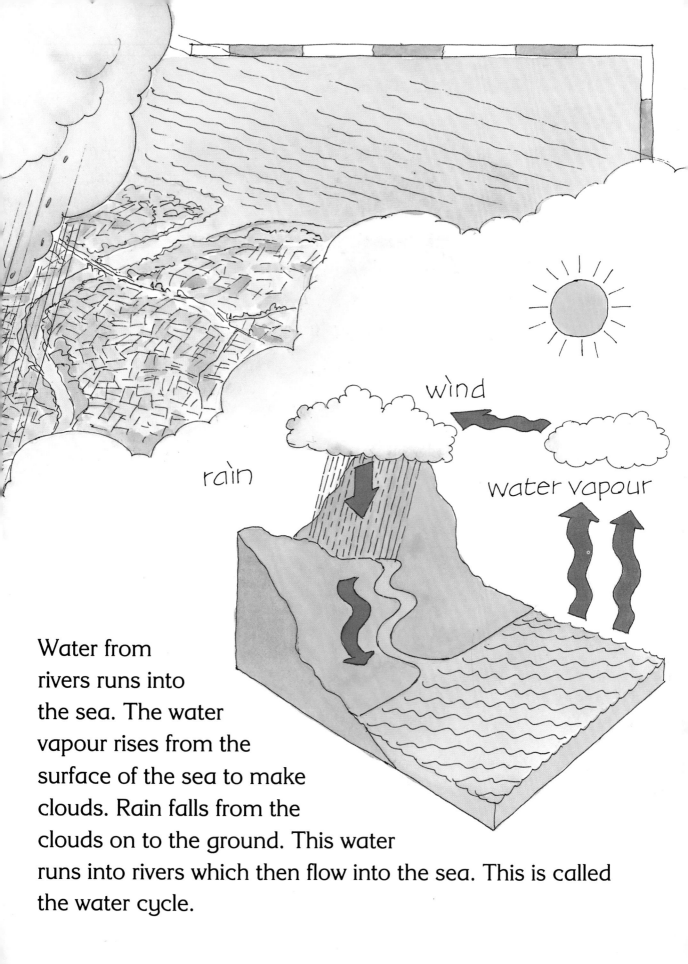

rain

wind

water vapour

Water from
rivers runs into
the sea. The water
vapour rises from the
surface of the sea to make
clouds. Rain falls from the
clouds on to the ground. This water
runs into rivers which then flow into the sea. This is called
the water cycle.

The Sun

Thank goodness! The Sun has come
out. In fact, the Sun never goes away.
The Earth travels round it constantly.
During the day, the Sun can be hidden by
clouds. At night, we can't see the Sun because our part of
the globe is turned away from it.
This is because the Earth itself is
slowly spinning, making day and night.

Sun

Earth travels round the Sun.

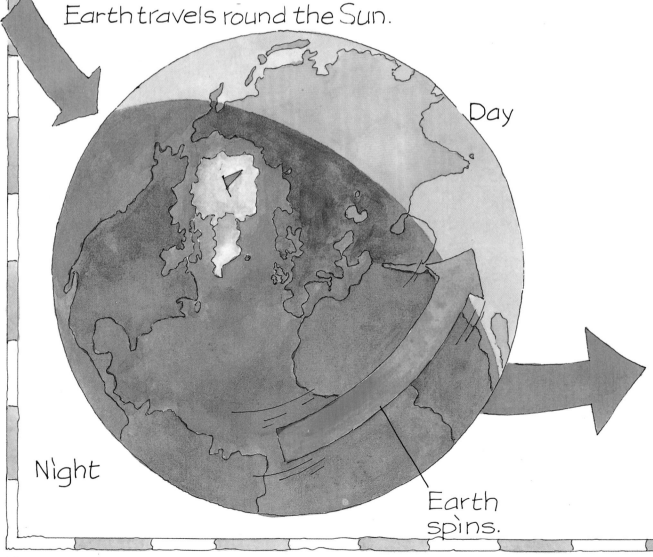

Day

Night

Earth
spins.

The Sun is a ball of flaming gas which gives us light, warmth and life. It is about one hundred times bigger than the Earth and more than 150 million kilometres away.

Sun and rain together make rainbows.

The white light from the Sun is split into seven main colours by the raindrops.

Heat from the Sun warms the ground. Then warmth from the ground heats the air above.

Sea breezes

As the air inside the balloon cools, the balloon slowly sinks to the ground. Harry and Ralph land by the sea.

It's windy by the sea. Harry knows that wind is moving air. He asks Fred about sea breezes.

Fred explains that air is similar to water because it can flow from place to place. When there is lots of air it's called high pressure. When there is less air it's called low pressure. On a hot day, warm air over the land rises, making an area of low pressure. Then air from a high pressure area, such as the air over the cool sea, blows in to fill its place. This makes a sea breeze.

All over the world winds are made when air from high pressure areas blows into low pressure areas.

Flashes and bangs

Remember those rain clouds? The wind has blown them towards Harry and Ralph. They shelter from the storm under Fred's boat.

FLASH! A flash of lightning is a huge electric spark made inside a big storm cloud.

The heat from the spark of lightning warms the
air which expands, or becomes bigger, and makes a loud
BANG! That's the thunder that Harry and Ralph hear.

More storms

Ralph blocks his ears. He doesn't like storms. Fred says he's lucky not to be at sea.

A really violent storm that builds up over tropical seas is called a hurricane. With winds of over 200 kilometres an hour, hurricanes can cause lots of damage.

Another sort of storm is called a tornado. Tornadoes are small, violent whirlwinds that suck up and destroy almost everything in their paths.

Many tornadoes happen in the mid western states of America.

Like Kansas, where Dorothy lives in *The Wizard of Oz?*

Snow

Ralph's favourite weather is snow. But it's the wrong time of year for snow. It has to be really cold before the water droplets in a cloud turn to ice crystals. The crystals join together to form snowflakes.

There can be snow all year round on high mountain tops and at the North and South Poles. In other places snow usually melts in the spring.

What's your favourite sort of weather? What's your favourite time of year? What is the weather like in spring, summer, winter and autumn where you live?

The weather forecast

Harry and Ralph watch the television to find out what the weather will be like. Weather forecasters collect information from weather stations all over the world. Some weather stations are on land, others are at sea. Weather balloons carry special weather instruments. Also weather satellites go round, or orbit, the Earth.

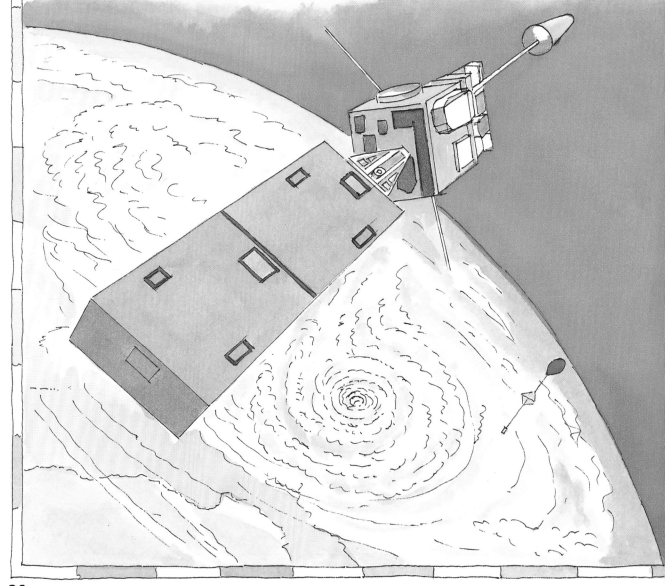

The weather stations give details of temperatures, rainfall, wind speed and direction. They can also tell what the air pressure is. This information is fed into a computer, which then shows the information on a map.

Using these maps, a forecaster can work out what the weather will be like for the next few days.

A weather station

Harry and Ralph have their own weather station at school. At the same time each morning and afternoon they record the temperature, the rainfall and the direction of the wind. Make a weather station for your garden or school and draw a chart that you can fill in each day.

The wind vane is made from a pencil and some plastic covered card.

There is a thermometer for measuring the temperature in the shade.

The rain gauge is made from two halves of a plastic bottle and a ruler.

And the wind is blowing from the south-west.

It's 20° Celsius today.

Index

This index will help you to find some of the important words in the book.